AYO'S **AWESOME** ADVENTURES IN

MOTHER CITY

www.worldbook.com

World Book, Inc.
180 North LaSalle Street
Suite 900
Chicago, Illinois 60601
USA

For information about other World Book publications, visit our website at www.worldbook.com or call 1-800-WORLDBK (967-5325).

For information about sales to schools and libraries, call 1-800-975-3250 (United States), or 1-800-837-5365 (Canada).

Library of Congress Cataloging-in-Publication Data for this volume has been applied for.

Ayo's Awesome Adventures
ISBN: 978-0-7166-3636-6 (set, hc.)

Ayo's Awesome Adventures in Cape Town: Mother City
ISBN: 978-0-7166-3639-7 (hc.)

Also available as:
ISBN: 978-0-7166-3650-2 (e-book)

1st printing July 2018

Staff

Writer: Jamie Diehm Moore

Executive Committee

President
Jim O'Rourke

Vice President and
Editor in Chief
Paul A. Kobasa

Vice President, Finance
Donald D. Keller

Vice President, Marketing
Jean Lin

Vice President, International Sales
Maksim Rutenberg

Vice President, Technology
Jason Dole

Director, Human Resources
Bev Ecker

Editorial

Director, New Print
Tom Evans

Managing Editor, New Print
Jeff De La Rosa

Series Editor
Nathalie Strassheim

Librarian
S. Thomas Richardson

Manager, Contracts & Compliance
(Rights & Permissions)
Loranne K. Shields

Manager, Indexing Services
David Pofelski

Digital

Director, Digital Product
Development
Erika Meller

Manager, Digital Products
Jonathan Wills

Graphics and Design

Senior Art Director
Tom Evans

Senior Visual Communications
Designer
Melanie Bender

Senior Web Designer/Digital
Media Developer
Matthew Carrington

Media Researcher
Rosalia Bledsoe

Senior Cartographer
John M. Rejba

Manufacturing/Production

Manufacturing Manager
Anne Fritzinger

Proofreaders
Mary Kieffer
Georgina Milsted

Contents

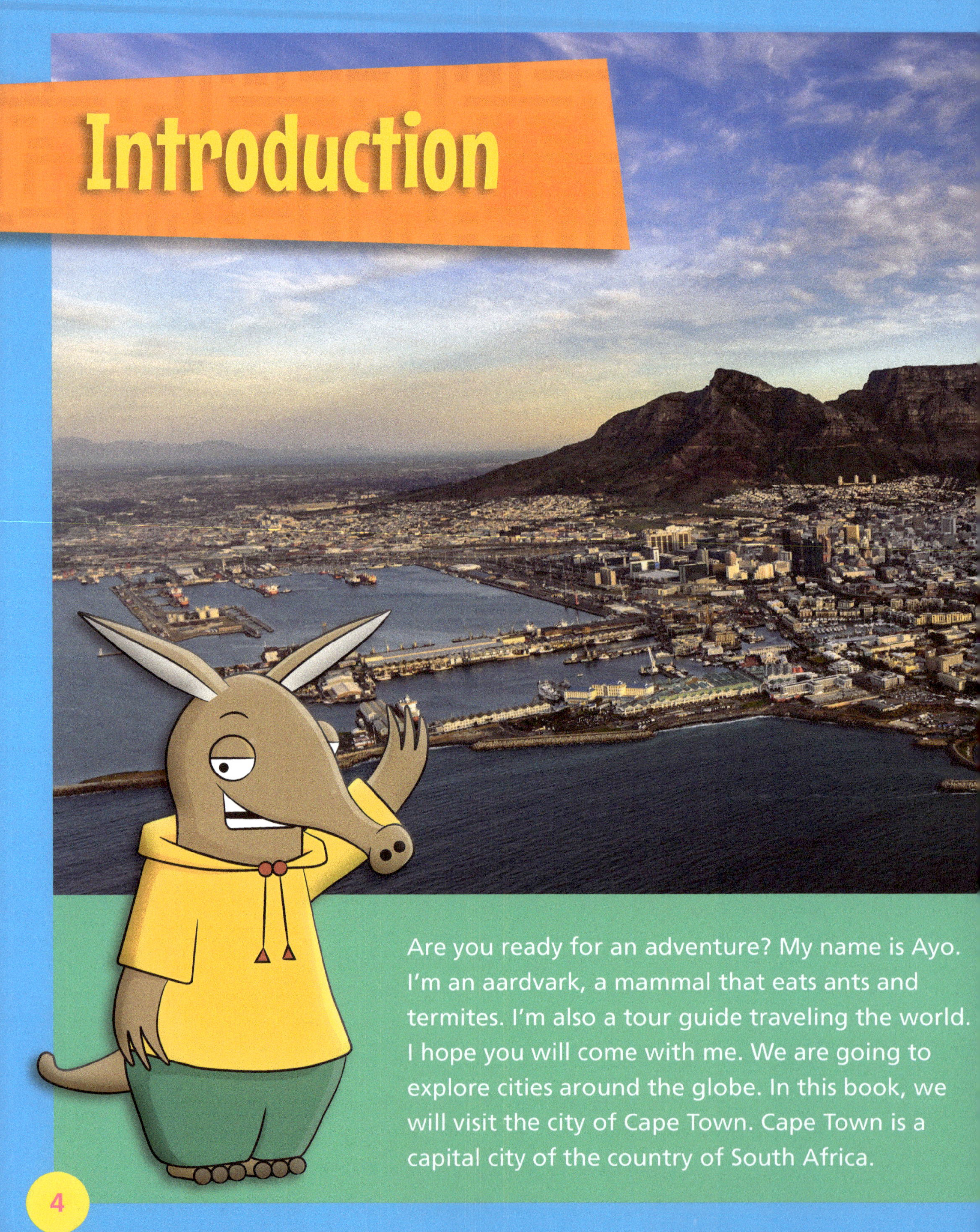

Are you ready for an adventure? My name is Ayo. I'm an aardvark, a mammal that eats ants and termites. I'm also a tour guide traveling the world. I hope you will come with me. We are going to explore cities around the globe. In this book, we will visit the city of Cape Town. Cape Town is a capital city of the country of South Africa.

Most countries have only one capital. South Africa has three: (1) Cape Town, (2) Pretoria, and (3) Bloemfontein. Each one is home to a different branch of government. Cape Town is the *legislative* capital—the place where people meet to make and change laws.

Cape Town is on the southwest coast of Africa, my home continent! Are you curious about my name? *Ayo* is an African word that means *joy.*

Some of the words we use on our travels may be new to you. If I can explain a word easily, I will do so right where you are reading. If I cannot explain a word easily, or if I use the word over and over again, I will put it in boldface (type that **looks like this).** All boldface words are defined in a glossary in the back of the book.

We may run into words you have not heard before. I'll slowly sound out words that may be strange to you. Here's an example. Many South Africans speak a language called Afrikaans. That's pronounced *af ruh KAHNS.*

I hope someday you can travel with your family to Cape Town. You can ask to see the places we visit in this book! Then you can be the tour guide for your parents and brothers and sisters.

Cape Town information

- Population: 3,740,026

- Founded: 1652

- Influences: Cape Town culture is influenced by different historical groups—Dutch settlers, *Huguenots* (French Protestants), British settlers, and slaves from South and Southeast Asia.

- Nickname: Cape Town is often called the *Mother City* because it was the first place in South Africa to be settled by Europeans.

South Africa information

- Climate: Warm, dry summers and cool, wet winters

- Money: Rand. One hundred cents equal one rand.

- Flag: The flag, adopted in 1994, represents the country's peoples coming together in unity.

flag of
South Africa

Table Mountain

I'm excited to show you around Cape Town. First, let's see the city from up high. We can check out the view from Table Mountain. Should we hike uphill or take the cable car? I have short legs, so I vote for cable car. It's like a little car that is pulled along thick wires called cables.

It's 900 feet (3,000 meters) to the top! The top is flat—like a table! From up here, we can see all of Cape Town. See how the city is squeezed between the mountains and Table Bay? Cape Town has grown a lot. It now reaches all the way to nearby False Bay, too.

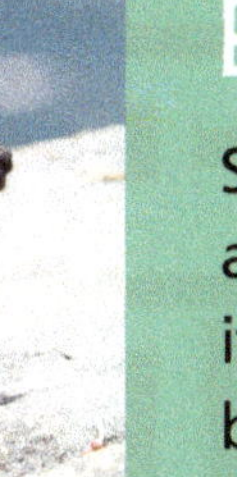

Elephant cousins

See that cute little animal warming itself on a sunny rock? It looks like a hamster, doesn't it? This animal is a rock hyrax (say *HY raks*), but everyone here calls them *dassies*. Its closest living relative is the elephant.

To the north, the ocean stretches beyond the city and Table Bay. To the south, there are mountains on the Cape **Peninsula.** A peninsula is an area of land almost surrounded by water. On one side of this peninsula is the Atlantic Ocean.

On the other side is False Bay. You might hear another name for the peninsula while you're here: the Cape of Good Hope. The city gets its name from this *cape.* A cape is a piece of land that sticks out into the ocean.

Table Bay

From Table Mountain, let's look toward downtown Cape Town. Do you see the body of water just beyond the downtown shoreline? That's Table Bay. In 1652, a Dutch ship captain named Jan van Riebeeck sailed into Table Bay. He worked for a big business called the Dutch East India Company.

The company brought spices and silk to Europe from the islands of Southeast Asia, once known as the East Indies. Table Bay was around the halfway point for ships making the journey. Riebeeck came to set

up a refreshment station—a place where sailors could stop to get fresh food and water, fix their boats, and rest. Van Riebeeck's job was to build a fort, plant a vegetable garden, and trade cattle with the native people who lived here. His refreshment station was the beginning of European settlement in South Africa.

Dutch sailors spent long weeks aboard their boats. They needed a break. You might need a break, too. Come on! Let's go play at the waterfront!

About 100 kinds of shark live in ocean waters off the coast of South Africa. At the Two Oceans Aquarium, we can get a close look at the ragged tooth shark. Its teeth look like needles! South Africans have a nickname for this shark: the raggie.

Victoria & Alfred Waterfront

Do you see the giant Ferris wheel? It's at the Victoria & Alfred Waterfront. Look at all the shops, restaurants, and people! It was crowded in the late 1800's, too. That's when many people arrived on ships to work in the area's gold and diamond mines. If I burrowed deep enough beneath South Africa, I would find lots of gold and diamonds! We can find out more about diamond mining at the waterfront diamond museum.

Who are Victoria & Alfred?

The waterfront is named after Queen Victoria of Great Britain, who lived from 1819 to 1901, and her second son. Alfred lived from 1844 to 1900. Dutch people founded Cape Town in 1652. The British took it over in the early 1800's.

samosas

Cape Town is a major port city, and the waterfront is a working harbor. We may see a ship being repaired or picking up fresh supplies. Speaking of supplies, I'm hungry! Let's get a snack at the food market.

These triangle-shaped pastries stuffed with veggies or meat look tasty. They are called *samosas (suh MOH suhz)*. Or how about an ostrich burger?

Robben Island

Let's hop on a ferry from the Victoria & Alfred Waterfront to Robben Island. Today, the island is a museum. But before that, it was a prison. The most famous prisoner here was Nelson Mandela. Why was he in jail? Mandela worked against a way of government called **apartheid** *(ah PAHRT hayt). Apartheid* is an **Afrikaans** word that means *separateness.* Under apartheid, laws kept white and nonwhite people separated. Apartheid laws were unfair and harmful to nonwhites.

Nelson Mandela was let out of prison in 1990. A year later, the last apartheid laws were *repealed* (canceled). People of any color could go to the same schools and live in the same neighborhoods. In 1994, nonwhites were allowed to vote for the first time. Nelson Mandela was elected president of South Africa.

Once our ferry reaches the island, we will get on a bus. On the bus tour, we'll see the prison building and *quarries* (rock mines) where the prisoners worked. If we're lucky, we'll see lots of animals, too! There aren't any aardvarks, but I hope we see tortoises, fur seals, and a type of antelope called the springbok.

Nelson Mandela
(1918-2013)

Sports

Have you ever been to a sports stadium where there is so much loud noise that you needed earplugs? You might need them if you go to a football game at Cape Town Stadium. *Football* here is the game people in Canada and the United States call *soccer*. The stadium is a huge building shaped like a bowl. It was built for the 2010 World Cup football tournament. Fans cheer with colorful plastic horns called *vuvuzelas (voo voo ZEHL uhz)*—thousands of them!

South Africa is a nation that loves sports. In Cape Town, football brings out the biggest crowds. Games called rugby and cricket are also popular. These used to be whites-only sports in South Africa. But that changed after **apartheid** ended in 1991.

If we wanted to catch a rugby match, we would head out to the suburb of Newlands. That's where Newlands Stadium is. But we would have to leave our vuvuzelas behind. They aren't allowed in the stadium. Newlands must be quieter than Cape Town Stadium.

South Africa's national anthem

combines songs of black Africans and white settlers. When you sing it, you speak five different languages! Each part is in a different language. Which of these languages do you usually speak?

- Xhosa *(KOH suh)*
- Zulu
- Sesotho *(seh SOH thoh)*
- **Afrikaans**
- English

Castle of Good Hope

Let's climb aboard a red sightseeing bus. It's a double-decker, with seating both inside and on top. It stops at the Castle of Good Hope and lots of museums downtown. I like to sit on the open top and take pictures along the way.

That large, yellow building is the castle. Do you notice anything unusual about the castle's shape? The castle was built in the shape of a *pentagon!* You remember pentagons from math class. They are shapes with five sides. Dutch settlers built the castle to defend their outpost against British invaders in the late 1600's. The castle held more than just soldiers. It was like a small town inside. There were apartments, a church, a bakery, offices, and even jail cells.

Do you need a rest? Let's find a shady place in the Company's Garden, near the castle, to relax and meet the friendly squirrels. We can buy a bag of food just for them. The Company's Garden was originally a vegetable garden. The garden was planted for the Dutch East India Company. The vegetables were for sailors on the company's trading ships.

The castle is the oldest **colonial** building in South Africa! Dutch colonists and their **slaves** finished building it in 1679.

Iziko South African Museum & Greenmarket Square

See the grand building at the end of the Company's Garden? That's the Iziko South African Museum. There are many interesting things inside for us to see.

We can learn how people from long ago lived in southern Africa. Their homes were huts, and their clothes were made of animal skins. Some of those skins came from antelopes. Remember the springbok we looked for on Robben Island? It is a kind of antelope. It has curvy horns and *springs* (jumps) into the air when threatened.

Now look up. The skeletons hanging from the ceiling are huge! They're not aardvark skeletons, are they? The biggest one is a blue whale skeleton. It is 67 feet (20.5 meters) long—longer than a school bus! Blue whales swim off the coast of Africa, but they aren't often seen.

After the museum, we can take a short stroll back toward the waterfront. It brings us to Greenmarket Square. Hey, it's bumpy underfoot. We're walking on **cobblestones,** a historic kind of pavement! The square has been here since 1696. It still holds one of Cape Town's oldest markets. Want to buy a souvenir—perhaps an African carving or a bead necklace?

District Six Museum

Let's take a short walk to the east side of town and the District Six Museum. The museum tells the story of a neighborhood that used to be on this exact spot.

Here's what happened. Long ago, people of different colors lived side by side in District Six. The neighborhood was alive with many types of food, music, and culture. But in 1966, during **apartheid,** a new law said only whites could live in District Six. More than 60,000 nonwhite people were forced to move. Bulldozers flattened their homes.

Families and friends who had lived in District Six for many years were sent to separate, sometimes faraway neighborhoods, called **townships.** Their tiny new homes were made of scrap metal sheets. Our museum guide has many stories to tell about living with no electric power, running water, or bathrooms. We can also see *reconstructions* of destroyed rooms. That means the rooms have been rebuilt to show what they used to look like.

A mixture of people

- Nearly half of **Capetonians** are black Africans of the Xhosa (*KOH suh*) people.

- About half more are Coloured, which means of mixed African, European, and Asian heritage.

- A much smaller number are white. These people have European ancestry, mostly from the Netherlands, the United Kingdom, France, and Germany. Some are called Afrikaners.

- The rest of the people are from other groups.

Spin Street & Slave Lodge

Follow me a few blocks to Spin Street. Aren't the buildings here fancy, with their arches and *gables* (roof features)? This style of building is called Cape Dutch.

Spin Street is a place where we can talk about a bad part of the city's history—slavery. We'll walk past a round marker on the ground. It marks the spot where the Slave Tree stood. Enslaved people arrived here on ships from other countries. They were sold beneath the tree's branches.

Around the corner is the Slave Lodge. It's the yellowish building at the end of the street. As many as 1,000 enslaved people could be kept here. Let's go inside. It doesn't look so bad in here now. But during the 1700's, it was a crowded, unpleasant place. Slavery was outlawed in the 1800's. This building became government offices and then a cultural museum. Some of the items on display here include slave handcuffs and chains. They help us to understand the story of slavery in Cape Town.

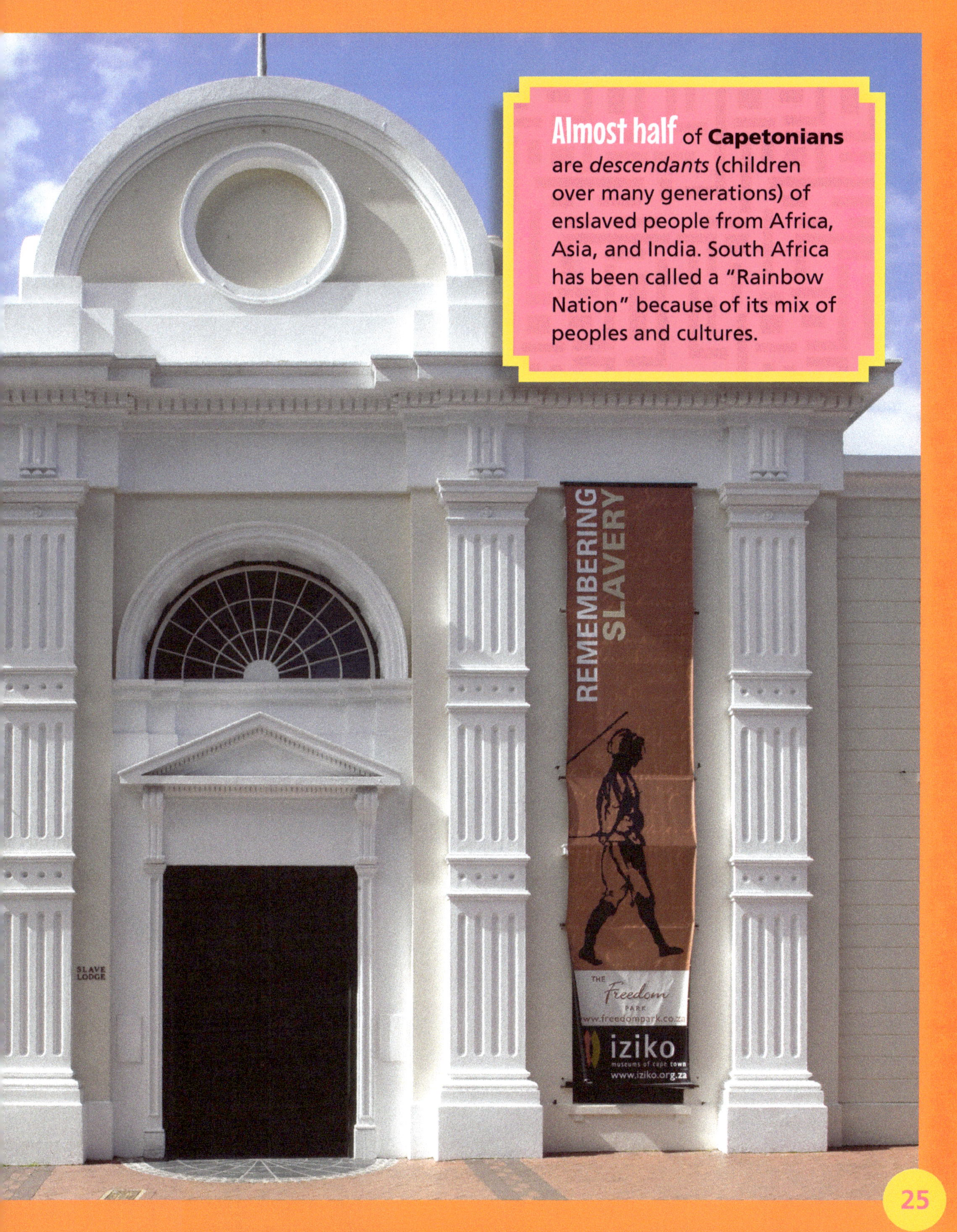

Almost half of **Capetonians** are *descendants* (children over many generations) of enslaved people from Africa, Asia, and India. South Africa has been called a "Rainbow Nation" because of its mix of peoples and cultures.

Bo-Kaap

Slopes rise all around downtown Cape Town, forming a natural bowl. Let's take a taxi to the slopes of Signal Hill and the neighborhood called Bo-Kaap. On the way, we'll pass a church called St. George's Cathedral. It has a giant colored glass window! St. George's has been called "the people's cathedral." It welcomed people of all skin colors even during **apartheid.**

You'll know we've reached Bo-Kaap when you start to walk on bumpy **cobblestone** streets. The houses here are painted bright pink, blue, orange, and green. Not all together, silly! Each house has a different color. It will be easy to spot a little brown aardvark against such bright colors.

Bo-Kaap is one of Cape Town's oldest neighborhoods. In the late 1700's, **slaves** from Southeast Asia moved here. These people became known as the Cape Malay. Many of them were Muslims who followed the religion of Islam. In 1794, they built the Auwal Mosque. A mosque is a Muslim house of worship. Now there are many more mosques. We can see the *minarets* when looking out over the city from these hilly streets. Minarets are prayer towers attached to mosques.

minaret

Dutch colonists
brought slaves to
Capetown from
Southeast Asia, where
they had already set up
colonies in the 1600's.

Let's eat!

Is it time to eat yet? I'm hungry! This snout smells the delicious scent of termites in *curry,* a spicy sauce. Oh, wait, maybe it's lamb curry! **Capetonians** enjoy many cultures and flavors. We can sample a little bit of everything.

In Bo-Kaap, let's look for *bobotie (buh BOO tee).* The Cape Malay are known for this dish. It's baked in a deep, round pan, like a pie. But it's made with ground-up lamb or beef and curry spice, with egg custard on top. Curry is a popular flavor in Asia and India, where many of Cape Town's Coloured people have their roots.

Mmmm, I smell a barbecue! In Cape Town, the word for barbecue is *braai (breye).* Many Capetonians like to cook a spicy coil of sausage on the braai. It's called *boerewors (BOO rih vohrs).*

What goes with barbecued meat? One traditional African side dish is *pap.* That's a cornmeal porridge with vegetables stirred in.

Snack time!

If you like beef jerky, you might like *biltong.* It's dried and salted meat. Kids in Cape Town take biltong to school for a snack. In the 1830's, Dutch people called Voortrekkers packed lots of biltong when they left Cape Town and moved inland.

boerewors
bobotie

Heart of Cape Town Museum

What do you want to be when you grow up? If you said "doctor" or "nurse," then you might find our next stop extra exciting.

We're going to the city's east side, to the Heart of Cape Town Museum. It's inside the Groote Schuur Hospital. What's so special about this hospital? The first successful human heart transplant surgery happened here. That means that someone got a heart from someone else!

We must remember to sign up for a tour. It's the only way to see the operating room where the surgery happened! Don't worry—we won't see any blood. But we will see all kinds of medical machines and instruments. Life-sized figures make the room look just like it did on the day of the surgery: December 3, 1967.

On that day, Dr. Christiaan Barnard made history. He put a donated heart from the body of a dead person into the chest of patient Louis Washkansky. The heart began to beat strongly. The doctor said in **Afrikaans,** "Dit gaan werk!" That means *It's going to work!*

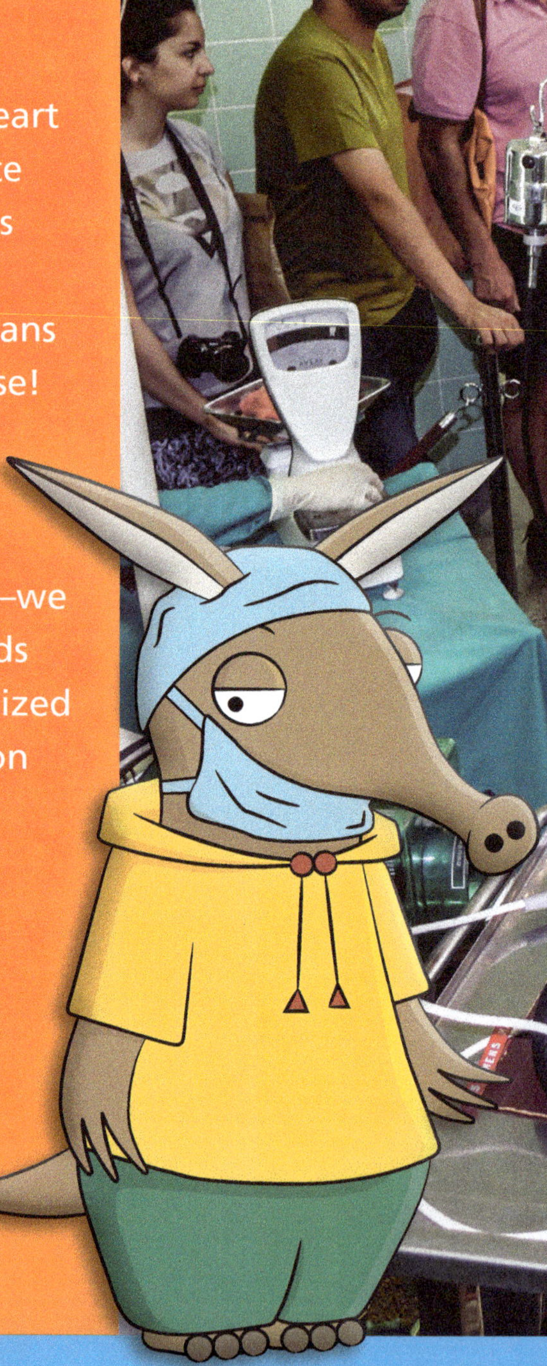

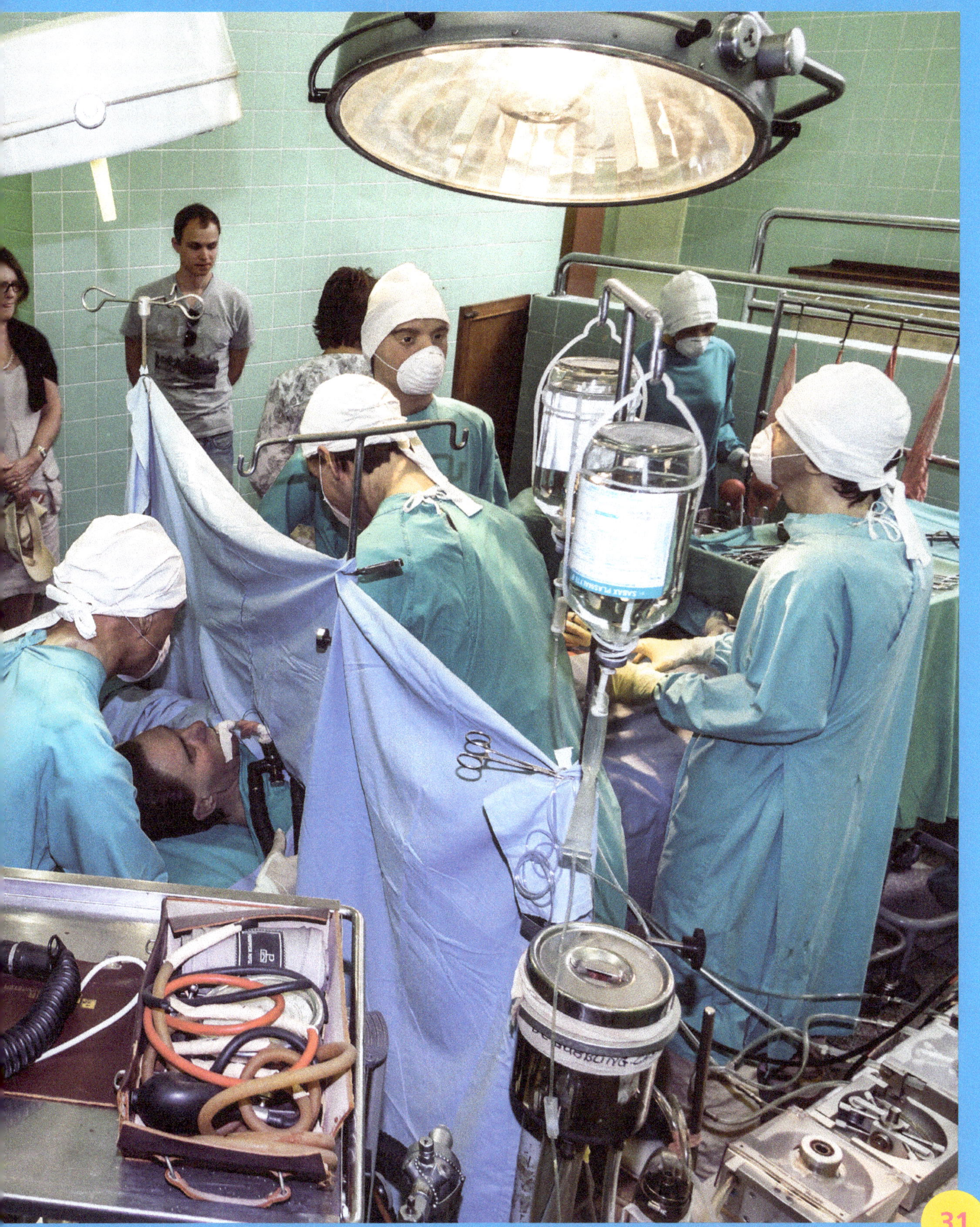

Kirstenbosch Botanical Garden

Ready to leave downtown and enjoy nature? I am! We don't have to go far. The red sightseeing buses will take us from the city center waterfront around to the other side of Table Mountain. On the eastern slopes is Kirstenbosch National Botanical Garden. This huge park is home to a special kind of environment called *fynbos (FYN baws)*. *Fynbos* comes from Dutch words meaning *fine bush*. Many kinds of small bushes and trees bloom in a burst of color in the South African

spring, from August to November.

The gardens here are full of life. Cape Crag lizards sleep on sunny rocks. Tortoises creep through the plants and over mountain slopes. In springtime, sugarbirds visit colorful flowers called pincushions. The birds have really long tails. They swoop down on the pincushions to snack on their *nectar* (a sugary liquid).

Oooo! Is that a yellow-haired sugar ant I smell? Slurp! Yum!

Hout Bay

Shall we explore farther down the **peninsula?** Let's take the bus to Hout Bay. The mountains drop right into the sea here.

The ocean water can be chilly on the cape's west side. We might be more comfy sunning ourselves on the white sand beach. Do I smell deep-fried fish and *chips* (French fries)? Mmmm. Several restaurants offer this treat.

Let's walk to the harbor, where the boats dock. Look! There's a Cape fur seal hanging around. Did you know thousands of fur seals live on Duiker Island just offshore? Some people call it Seal Island. We can take a boat tour to see them. Young seals, called pups, are born in early December (that's early summer in South Africa).

If you visit on a weekend, take a stroll through the Bay Harbour Market. Local bands play live music that keeps my claws tapping. Have you found a souvenir yet? People who make all kinds of crafts have something to show you in their stands.

Hold on tight!

Chapman's Peak Drive—the road from Hout Bay to nearby Noordhoek—clings to the edge of a seaside cliff. It curves more than 100 times. Maybe we'll see whales in the ocean below.

Beaches

Would you believe Cape Town has 72 beaches? Many South African families like to go to the beach. They swim and play in the sun.

It sure is windy on the cape's west coast and in Table Bay! The beaches here are known for surfing. Let's go watch surfers, wind surfers, and kite surfers wiggle into their wetsuits on Blaauwberg Beach. If we stick around long enough, we might see—and smell!—people barbecuing **boerewors** right on the beach.

The Atlantic Ocean beaches are exciting, but the water can be chilly. My favorite beaches are on False Bay, southeast of downtown Cape Town. Ocean currents bring warmer waters into False Bay, making it more pleasant to swim there.

Muizenberg Beach is a fun place to swim, learn to surf, or just dig in the sand with your claws. Do you need to change into your swimsuit? You can do that in these brightly colored shacks, called "bathing boxes." They're an old British tradition.

False Bay got its name

long ago from sailors. They were disappointed when they sailed into this bay thinking it was Table Bay. After their long journey from the East Indies, they were ready for the refreshment station!

surfing at
Long Beach
Muizenberg
Beach

Kalk Bay

I love the east coast of the Cape **Peninsula.** Look at those mountains above the town of Kalk Bay. Sometimes, you can see schools of fish in the bay's clear waters. Follow me to the fishing harbor. I can tell that we are getting close. I can hear the cry of seagulls, and the air smells fishy.

People sell freshly caught fish right out of the boats! I think the seals are hoping that they will drop a silvery snoek (*snook*). Snoek are a fish eaten smoked, *braaied* (barbecued), dried, or salted. Which way sounds good to you?

In the early 1800's, Kalk Bay and

nearby Simon's Town were whaling towns. People made a living by hunting right whales. They turned the whale's fat, or blubber, into oil to be burned in lamps. The whales were hunted almost to *extinction*. There would have been no more right whales in the world. Whaling is outlawed now. Keep an eye out for whales from June to October. That's when right whales return to the warm waters of False Bay each year. Why? To *calve* (have babies)!

Let's visit Simon's Town next.

Simon's Town

A little farther down the False Bay coast is Simon's Town. Guess who it was named after—a man named Simon! In the late 1600's, Simon van der Stel was governor of the Cape Colony. That was the name of the Dutch settlement back then. In the mid-1700's, the Dutch East India Company started to anchor its boats in this harbor every winter. It was more sheltered from storms than the Table Bay harbor.

Let's go check out the stone storehouses from the original 1740's shipyard. Now the shipyard is a base for the South African Navy. Can you spot the big gray ships at the dock?

A quick taxi ride will take us to see black-footed penguins at Boulders Beach. Hey! Do you hear that? "Hee haw … hee haw!" These penguins sure sound like donkeys, don't they? They're a lot louder than aardvarks! Several thousand penguins live around the beach's giant granite boulders. Follow me across the boardwalk and out onto the sand so we can get a closer look … but not too close. The penguins are *endangered*. That means they are in danger of going extinct. (You know what that means— there wouldn't be any more of them.) They also bite!

Cape Point

We'll end our tour at the southern tip of the **peninsula:** Cape Point. I love to look out from the lighthouses here. But how do we get up to them? We can ride the funicular (*fyoo NIHK yuh luhr*) railway. A funicular railway has two cars connected by a cable. As one car goes downhill, it helps to pull the other one up. The older lighthouse is near the funicular stop. We can walk by trail to the newer lighthouse. The newer one was built in 1914 and is the most powerful on the coast of South Africa. Every 30 seconds, it flashes three times.

The Cape of Good Hope was once called the Cape of Storms. Bad weather made it hard for sailors to steer their ships around the cape. Lots of rocks hide below the water's surface, too. See the waves breaking on them? At least 26 ships have wrecked here. On the Shipwreck Trail, we can see one that ran aground and is still on the beach.

Just think—nothing but ocean separates us from Antarctica!

The funicular is named the *Flying Dutchman*, after a legendary ghost ship. Long ago, an entire ship is said to have disappeared while sailing around the cape. Legend says the ghostly ship and her crew still haunt these waters.

Table Mountain
Bo-Kaap
Beaches
Kirstenbosch Botanical Gardens

Cape Point
Thanks for exploring
Cape Town with me.
I hope to see you
soon!

Ayo

Glossary

Afrikaans *(af ruh KAHNS)* A language made by many groups of people who lived or settled in South Africa. Those groups include Dutch, French, and German settlers, native people, and enslaved people from Asia and Africa.

apartheid *(ah PAHRT hayt)* A set of South African laws that kept people of different races separate. It sorted people into different groups—black, white, Coloured (mixed race), and Asian. These groups were separated in all areas of life, including school, homes, jobs, and transportation.

boerewors *(BOO rih vohrs)* Spicy sausage shaped into a coil

Capetonian *(kayp TOH nee uhn)* A person who lives in Cape Town

cobblestone *(KOB uhl stohn)* Rounded bricks used for making streets

colony, colonial *(KOL uh nee, kuh LOH nee uhl)* A colony is a settlement started by people outside their native land. It is ruled by their home country.

peninsula *(puh NIHN suh luh)* An area of land that is nearly surrounded by water. Peninsulas are usually long, narrow strips of land.

slave *(slayv)* A person who is owned by another person. Slaves work without pay. Slaves are often brought against their will from one place or country to another.

township *(TOWN shihp)* In South Africa, an area on the edge of the city set aside for blacks to live in under apartheid. Townships were known for their poor housing, and lack of electricity and running water.

Acknowledgments

Cover   © James Jones Jr., Shutterstock
Ayo artwork by Matthew Carrington

4-9   © Shutterstock
10-11   © Richard Van Der Spuy, Dreamstime
12-13   © Shutterstock
14-15   © Robert Harding, Alamy Images; © Mark Reinstein, Shutterstock
16-17   © Robyn Gwilt, Shutterstock; © Patrick Allen, Dreamstime
18-19   © Shutterstock
20-21   © Blaize Pascall, Alamy Images; © Shutterstock
22-23   © Jeffrey Greenberg, UIG/Getty Images
24-25   © Antony Souter, Alamy Images
26-27   © iStockphoto; © Shutterstock
28-29   © Shutterstock
30-31   © Jeffrey Greenberg, UIG/Getty Images
32-33   © Shutterstock
34-35   © Pete Oxford, Minden Pictures/SuperStock; © Neil Bradfield, Shutterstock
36-37   © Shutterstock
38-39   © iStockphoto
40-41   © Peter Titmuss, Dreamstime; © Neil Bradfield, Shutterstock
42-43   © Holger Karius, Dreamstime; © Grobler du Preez, Shutterstock; © Marisa Estivill, Shutterstock

Index

For further reading

Books

deNapoli, Dyan. *The Great Penguin Rescue.* New York: Free Press/Simon & Schuster, 2010.

Denenberg, Barry. *Nelson Mandela: "No Easy Walk to Freedom."* New York: Scholastic, 2014.

Eyewitness Travel South Africa. 2011.

Fodor's South Africa. 2015.

Websites

Animals
http://kids.nationalgeographic.com/

South Africa facts
https://www.natgeokids.com/za/discover/geography/countries/facts-about-south-africa/

How the heart works
https://www.brainpop.com/health/bodysystems/heart/

Apartheid
https://www.brainpop.com/socialstudies/worldhistory/apartheid/

Earth Science (ocean)
http://ocean.si.edu/ocean-news/currents-waves-and-tides-ocean-motion